eleven whispers

(a rhyming journey)

by shelby glows

Library of Congress Data is available.

ISBN: 978-0-9908463-4-5

Published by
Glowworks Production, LLC
1314 E Las Olas Blvd #1830
Ft. Lauderdale, FL 33301

shelby glows
www.shelbyglows.com
Instagram: @shelbyglows

Art and Design by C.A. Arroyo
www.eyetail.com

though our purpose is unclear,
still we all do matter here.

in a flat on monarch street
lived a girl you'd want to
meet... she had the most
creative mind, of the rarest
sort of kind...

as she slept she dreamed of
things like castles and
giraffes with wings

1 sorbet sky

i walked along the setting sun
and played with dolphins on my run
we swam through fields of marigold
such amusing stories that they told

about how they would tease the whales
and swirl around them, poke their tails
the purple orange sorbet sky
we took to air so we could fly

we met a mystic unicorn
that sang a strange melodic song
she whispered that there was a dance
on northstar, so we took a chance

i rode with her and what i saw
were zebras drinking at the bar
they had bowties and top hats, too
and told how they escaped the zoo

a sea of rainbow ballroom gowns
waltzed merrily to ballroom sounds
turtles carried trays of cake
red velvet heaven on my plate

i got so tired, so they said
go take a nap on that cloud bed
i smiled as i fell asleep
content with lucid memories

a sudden piercing alarm sound
startled and woke me back to now
disappointed to be in my room
i wanted the dance to resume

i hit the snooze and closed my eyes
back to the star and sorbet skies

she woke up feeling
uninspired, hoping to
reclaim her fire.
then she started
to inquire...

this is what she heard

2 obscurity

fading til i can't be seen
fearing who's replacing me
mundane tasks that dull my dreams
being average haunting me

chasing my significance
til i lose my own essence
validation eases doubt
false opinions have no clout

in the end we fade away
all that matters here today
is that we love that we laugh
and the gifts we give away

good morning dog.
good morning cat.

what should we do about
all that?

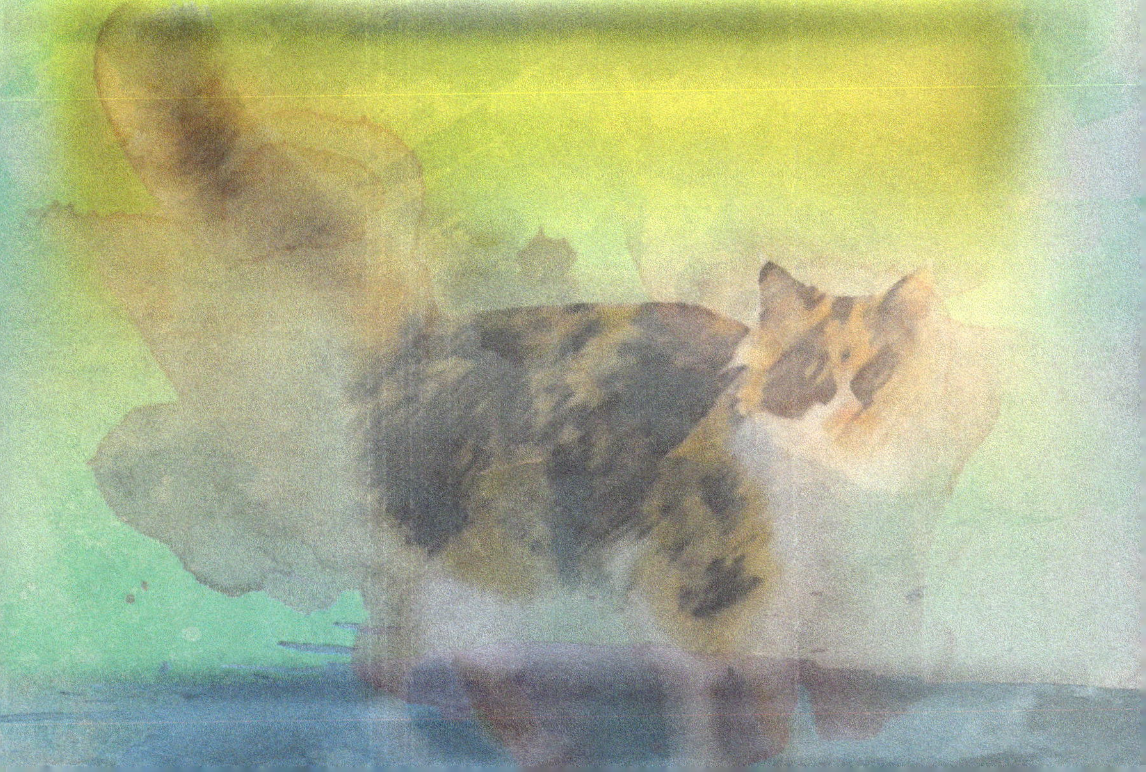

3 cat sage

caterpillar said that he
would like to fly away so free
and bluebird wanted to soar high
as eagles flying in the sky

the bumble bee had other dreams
to make honey to please the queen
the owl hooted all night long
and hoped someone would hear his song

the cat i think is life's true sage
she seems content to nap and play
attention is not what she seeks
no care is given if you speak

she's happy in her solitude
and eases through her many moods
can play for hours with just a string
and rarely asks for anything

she does not occupy her day
upset things did not go her way
and seems to know her purpose here
is cherished purrs and being near

dog, you don't seem to care.

you want to go out?

let's get some air,
take a walk away from here.

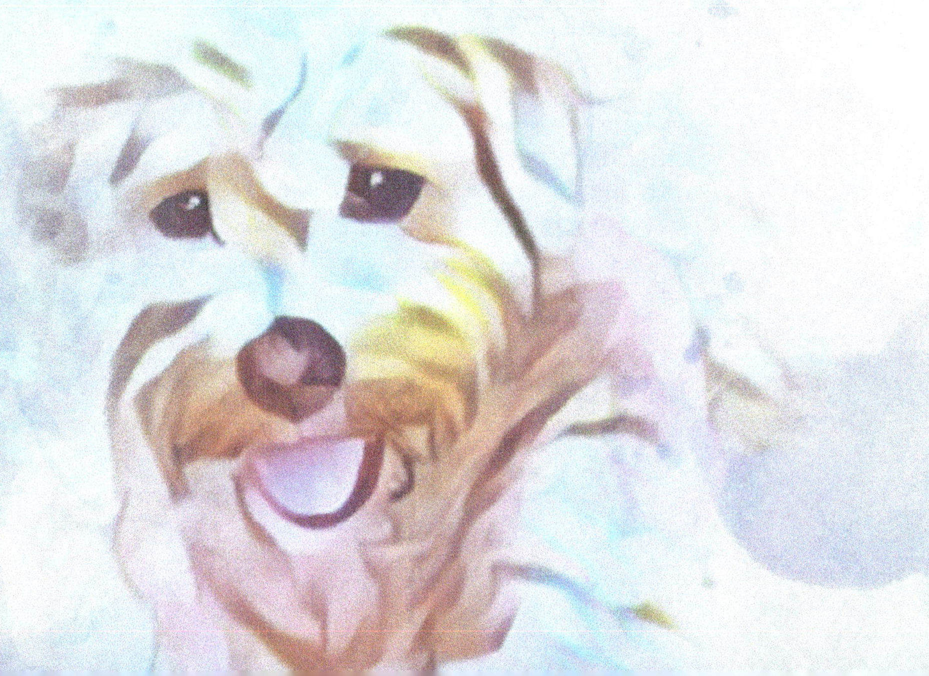

4 dog sonnet

happy feet are muddy paws
wagging tails and door mark claws
bathtime shakes and things you break
rainy walks - i wish you'd talk

bone collection - grand affection
scruffy face and squirrel chase
jumping up 'cause need a hug
curled up in your favorite rug

chewed up shoes mean don't go out
take me with you or i'll pout
perked up ears that say i care
follow you to anywhere

lonely whines mean want more time
to be together - ALWAYS THINE

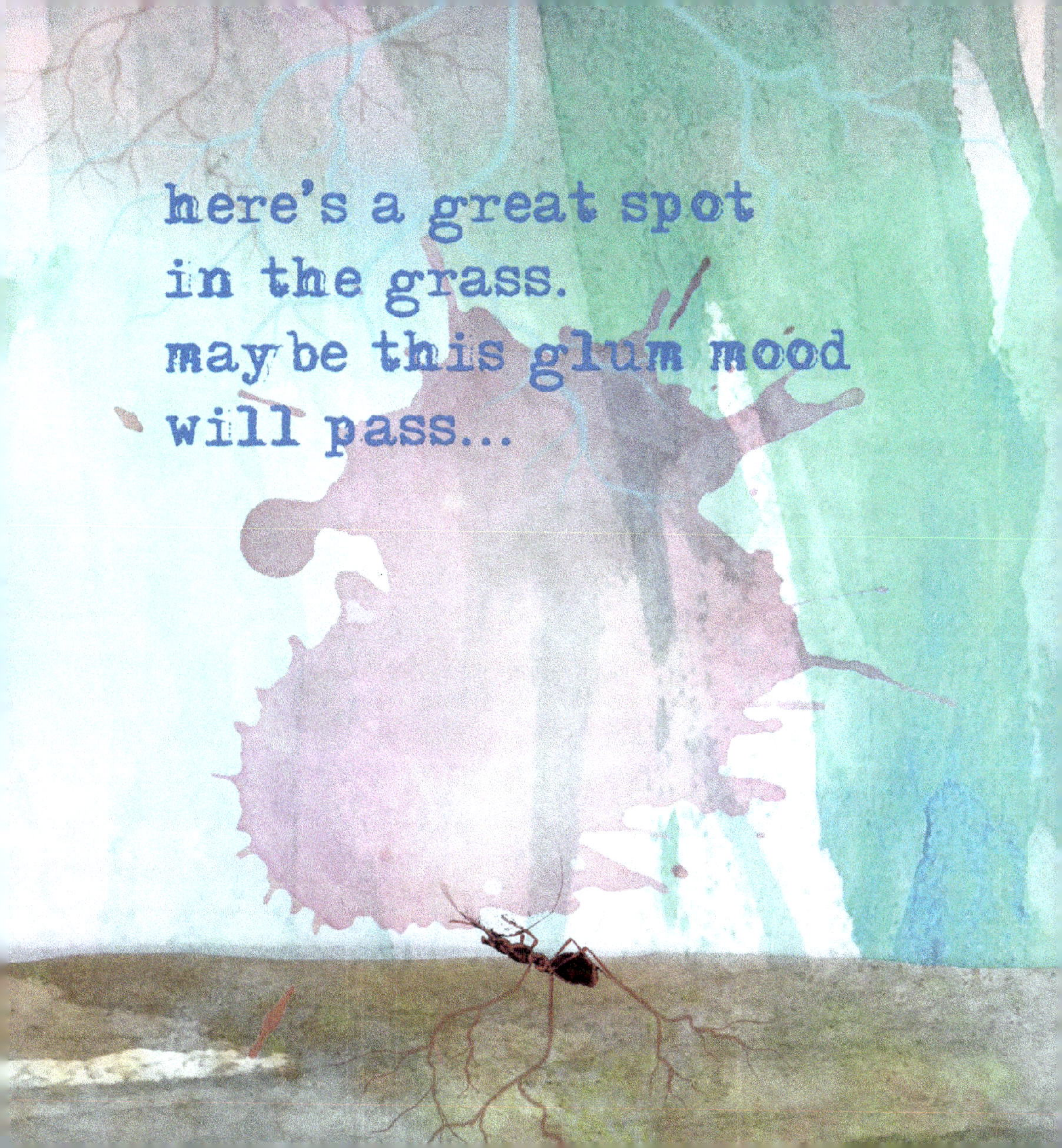

here's a great spot
in the grass.
maybe this glum mood
will pass...

5   the ant

i noticed a brown ant today
she persevered and toiled away
to carry off a biscuit crumb
and bring it back for all of them

it was a load three times her size
and yet she gave it all her tries
after she dropped it at the nest
she went back to get all the rest

this rigorous activity
was constant in the colony
i pondered in the setting sun…
do you think ants have any fun?

i think
this is all in vain,

striving for
an endless gain.

maybe the
trees can explain.

6 counsel of trees

when you don't know what you should do
go find a quiet place to stew
and sit beside the wisest tree
be still and ask so quietly

divulge to this tree all your strife
confess what is wrong in your life
then sit still and don't make a sound
listen to answers so profound

the wisdom of a thousand years
will be heard in your inner ears
the answers are the purest truth
that will identify the root

her branches exude perfect love
and understanding from above
compassion and respect unfold
trees keep the secrets that you told

they harbor so much truth to share
they're grateful that someone does care
so when you don't know where to turn
and things are very uncertain

try talking to a tree you know
and you will never be alone

i heard
something
in the air

you go chase,
i'll stay
right here...

and listen

7 yes

the only way to see what's clear
is close your eyes and slowly stare
until there is a nothingness
so things can come into focus

confusion will evaporate
and you can start to see your fate
dilemmas seem like child's play
and obstacles just go away

the clouds part and you see a star
that points the way from where you are
decisions are no longer there
because the path is crystal clear

the finish line is not in sight
but next steps point you left or right
the end is shifting constantly
and that is why you cannot see

the only thing that's real is NOW
we need not worry for the how
the next move like a game of chess
reveals itself in the stillness

resounding, solemn whisper….YES

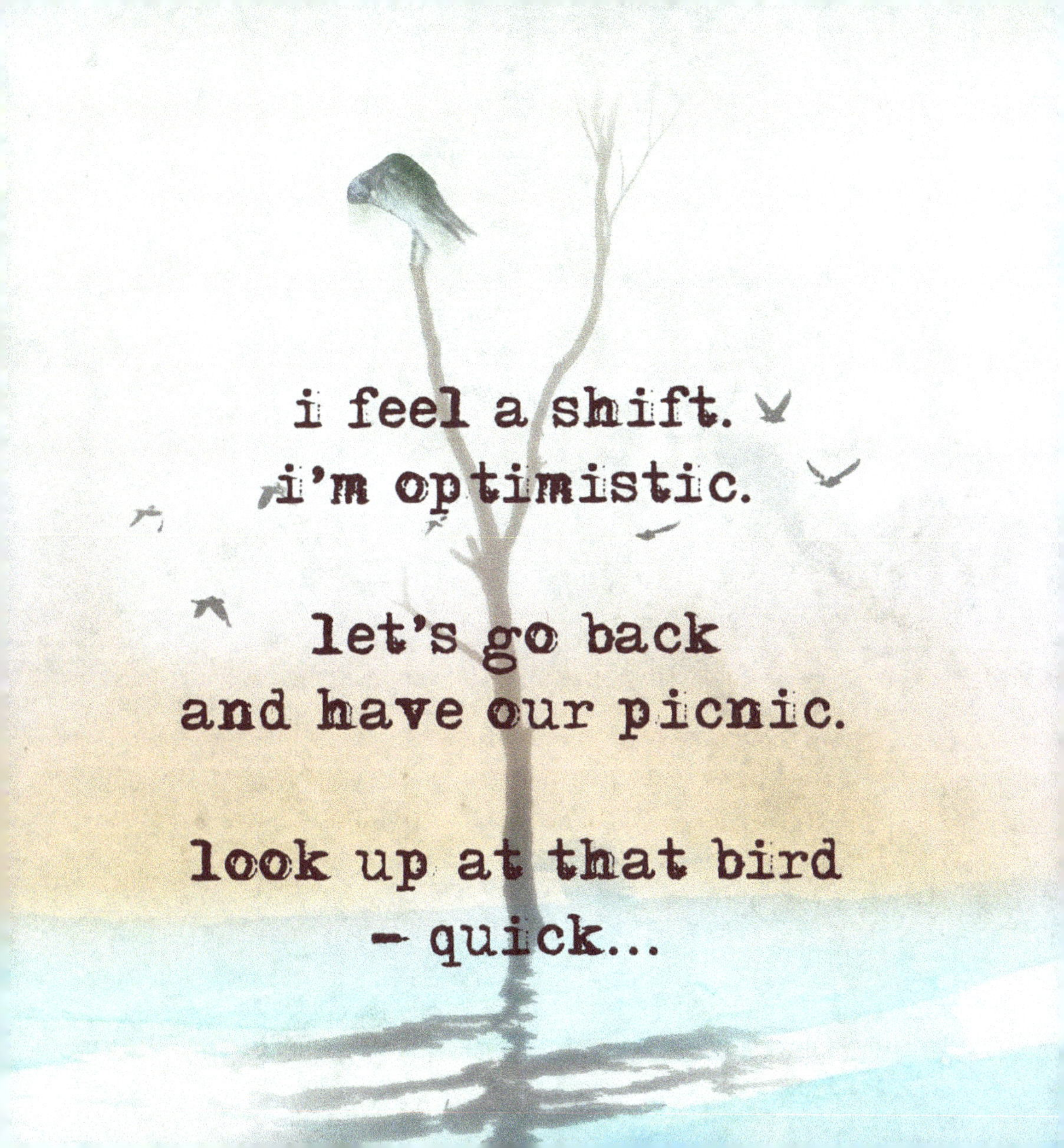

i feel a shift.
i'm optimistic.

let's go back
and have our picnic.

look up at that bird
- quick...

8 soar

everyone is scared sometimes
when they really want to fly
i'm not ready…wait….not yet
this could be my last regret

all the other birds now soar
maybe i can try once more
scared how vast the endless sky
but i really want to try

sitting in my nest so tall
way down there looks far to fall
have you ever felt this way?
want to go, but want to stay?

things are
getting clearer now.

It's not what –
it's simply how.

9 duckling

palm trees dancing in the wind
like cheering pom poms wavering
raindrop puddles rushing by
warm outside. it's quick to dry

baby ducks learning to swim
every day i watch for them
puddles become mini pools
for ducks to learn at swimming school

small webbed feet that splash about
mom duck says, time to get out
three yellow fluffs follow her lead
but one speckled fluff refused to heed

he swam around and ducked his head
she paused and called him to be led
the other ducks scurried about
but speckled fluff would not get out

he splashed about for two more tries
as mom duck feigned a swift goodbye
he realized that he could not yet
survive alone without regret

his pure defiance made me smile
reflecting how i've walked my mile
independent and headstrong
but helping hands that came along

to pick me up when i fell down
and couldn't even make a sound
i think we need to test our wings
try our luck and see new things

but no one can survive alone
this is what the ducks have shown.

this day has been a delight.

i'm inspired now to write.

let's head back before it's
night.

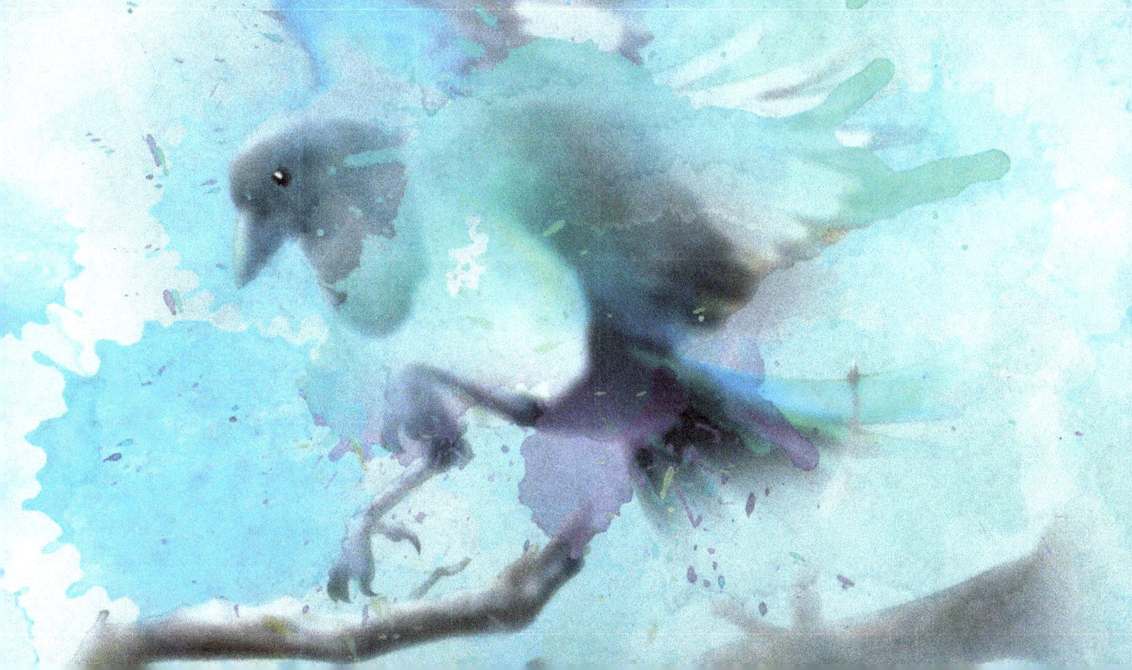

10 magpie

magpie swooped down by my head
want to play with me? i said
followed me from tree to tree
what do you want me to see?

stopped and stared - four eyes connect
then she tried to give a peck
off i went to walk away
down she came. are we at play?

round my head, buzz in my ear
what you want is just not clear
stop again for one long stare
oh, eggs are near is what you fear

such devoted bravery
small magpie mom fearless indeed
imagine what our love could do
if we were half as brave as you.

hello, cat. how are you?
want to hear what we've been
through? while i tuck you
both in bed, here's my new
poem in my head

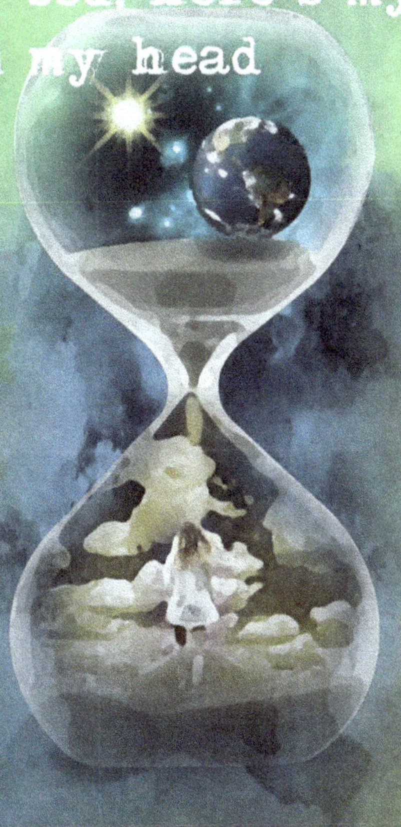

11 hours

life is like a fresh new day
we come here to grow and play
eating berries, drinking wine
up at seven, now it's nine

walking through the city streets
many people we do meet
intertwining lives are made
'til the sun begins to fade

new adventures, things to see
places that we have to be
dinnertime and getting late
it is now quarter to eight

families that we create
delicacies on our plate

summer love and heartbreak too
teaching how to tie a shoe
furry friends to romper with
that comfort and our spirits lift

evening comes and we look back
things we did and our impact
bedtime stories that we wrote
readings of our favorite quotes

turning off the bedroom light
as we now drift off to night
this has been a magic day
we would really like to stay

midnight and the moon is high
now it's time to say goodbye
one last thing before we go
we will meet again.. i know

love,
shelby glows

notes

notes

notes